COME SMILE WITH ME

Ottawa Valley Yarns

written by
Bernie Bedore
and
Wanda Lynn Butler

Illustrated by Bill Buttle

Quarry Press

from the heart of
The Valley!
W Lynn Butler
&
Bernie Bedore
1990

The publisher thanks The Canada Council and the Ontario Arts Council for assistance in publishing this book.

CANADIAN CATALOGUING IN PUBLICATION DATA

Bedore, Bernie, 1923– and Butler, Wanda Lynn, 1952–
Come smile with me

ISBN 0-919627-85-4

1. Tales — Ottawa River Valley (Quebec and Ont.).
2. Legends — Ottawa River Valley (Quebec and Ont.).
I. Butler, Wanda Lynn. II. Buttle, Bill. III. Title.

PS8553.E31C64 1990 398.23'27138 C90-090167-5
PR9199.3.B43C64 1990

Design and imaging by *ECW Type & Art*, Oakville, Ontario.

Distributed in Canada by the University of Toronto Press, 5201 Dufferin Street, Downsview, Ontario M3H 5T8, and in the United States of America by Bookslinger, 502 North Prior Avenue, St. Paul, Minnesota 55104.

Published by *Quarry Press, Inc.*, P.O. Box 1061, Kingston, Ontario K7L 4Y5 and P.O. Box 348, Clayton, New York 13624.

CONTENTS

FOREWORD

The stories and yarns in *Come Smile with Me* were first written some years ago by Bernie Bedore and now are rewritten in collaboration with Wanda Lynn Butler and enhanced by the illustrations of Bill Buttle. These three "B's" — Bedore, Butler, Buttle — have conspired artistically to capture in words and pictures the distinctive humor of the Ottawa Valley way of life. They have also immortalized in print some of the legendary Ottawa Valley storytellers — yarn spinners like Dinny O'Brien, Paddy Garvey, and the larger-than-life Johnny Coulonge — while showing the many ways of telling a story well.

So, *Come Smile with Me* is at once local history, folklore, popular biography, and a storytelling primer — but best of all, the book is funny. Now meet the creators of *Come Smile with Me* who invite you to smile with them.

Steeped in the heart of The Ottawa Valley, Bernie Bedore has an abiding love for its people. He also knows them damn well. He himself is widely known through The Valley and across the nation as the creator of the mythical character Big Joe Mufferaw, Canada's gentle giant. And Bernie's "Wee Lads," Ottawa Valley leprechauns who inhabit Mount St. Patrick near Dacre, have long been a source of delight for children young and old.

Bernie grew up in the Central Hotel in Arnprior, a much fabled "stopping place" and "settin' room" his parents managed. Here he met the storytelling giants of The Valley and learned their ways. Here he also started a life-long habit of collecting tales, yarns, jokes, soothsayings — which he has transformed and retold in such books, plays, and songs as *Tall Tales of Joe Mufferaw, Yonder Lies the Valley, The Shanty*, and now *Come Smile with Me*, his crowning achievement. Bernie is a master storyteller, rightly called The Bard of the Ottawa Valley, who has passed on his special way of telling a tale to Wanda Lynn Butler.

Descendant of a proud French family, Lynn Butler's heritage includes a blend of Welsh, Irish, and Dutch ancestry. As a result, she has a deep Ottawa Valley appreciation for the many ethnic origins of her country.

A simple phone call to Lynn, regarding a point of copyright, brought her together with Bernie Bedore. At the time, Lynn was the editor of *The Byline*, the newsletter of the Canadian Authors Association's Ottawa Branch. An immediate realization of their common interests and goals resulted in a very effective writing team.

Lynn majored in Art History and English at Ottawa's Carleton University. Her appreciation of storytelling, along with her own writing skills, quick active mind, sharpened by a ready wit and love of the humorous side of life, bloomed when she and Bernie combined their talents to produce *Come Smile with Me.* Together, they have continued to explore many other delightful avenues of their partnership in poetry, fiction, mythology, tall tales, lore, and legend. Indeed, several more Valley books are ready for publication.

Bill Buttle is a Valley lad "born and bred" in Pakenham. His father was one of the last country doctors whose practice extended throughout Pakenham, Waba, White Lake, and Arnprior.

Bill graduated in Dentistry from the University of Toronto in 1962. He practiced in Ottawa for five years, then in Arnprior for 21 years, ending his career as a dentist in 1988.

Bill had always aspired to try his hand as a cartoonist. He began with local papers, then his work was picked up by the Thomson newspaper chain and appeared coast-to-coast. He later moved to syndication with Miller Features, affiliated with Universal Press Syndicate. His well-known comic strip, *Two's a Crowd*, appears in many North American newspapers.

When Bernie Bedore approached him to illustrate *Come Smile with Me*, Bill agreed to take a crack at it. Bill's talented pen and easy-going manner resulted in the chuckle-sparking character interpretations that bring the anecdotes in *Come Smile with Me* to life.

INTRODUCTION: "TASTE THE SMILE"

With a fond heart I remember my childhood growing up in the Ottawa Valley, especially my schoolin' in the art of storytelling by the colorful characters who gathered 'round the old stove in the settin' room and bellied up to the bar in my home, Arnprior's old Central Hotel. You see, my parents managed the hotel, and the public rooms became both my playground and classroom where I sat at the foot of the master storytellers of the Ottawa Valley.

The old, retired shanty lads would gather in the settin' room after the evening meal, wearing their tall black hats, string ties about their necks. Their crooked pipes filled the air with a blue haze. They beckoned to a much younger Bernie Bedore, "Come here, little Mufferaw, sit on me knee and I'll tell you a story."

"I mind one time, I was up on the Kipaway for George Graham . . ." and away would go the storytelling, one story after another. Sometimes the old lads would run out of tales, but they'd never let on.

A hotel brat I guess I was. I learned a lot of things I wouldn't have if I hadn't met so many people of various ethnic origins, attitudes, ways of life, educational levels, and general individual peculiarities. Back in those days, people were individualists. They didn't follow the herd like cattle as the majority does now.

Maybe that's why I retained a sense of individuality. That's one thing I hope I never lose. When I see results of the brush of sameness across the land it hurts me inside. People are homogenized, so ready to follow, to keep up with the next one, to work hard to get more than the next lad — and for what?

OLD
FACE-
FULL

"Take 'er as she comes, and enjoy 'er," is what the old lads would say as they pulled a rickety old chair or a bench across the bare pine floor to the home made pine table. "To each his own" was another saying — "You go your way, I'll go mine." "I've got plenty, any more would only go to waste." "What's the use pilin' 'er up, she only gets in the way." "All I need's enough to bury me" and "You can't take 'er with yuh, there's no pockets in a shroud."

Here are a few of the tales I heard and some of the antics I watched while growing up with these "old lads" who always greeted me with the warm, open welcome heard throughout the Ottawa Valley, "Gidday! How are yuh?"

With the same good cheer I invite you to "Taste the Smile":

Lads don't sit around
and tell stories now,
as much as they used to.

But I always figure
if you can't spin
an odd yarn
and have a wee chuckle
now and then . . .

You're not gettin'
much out of life.

So sit a spell
yarn a bit
Let's think of
happy things
as we sit.

Taste the smile
each day can bring.

"I MIND ONE TIME"

Wee Tales from across The Valley

PREFACE

Lads here and there across The Valley have favorite "wee" jokes they invariably squeeze into a conversation. "Say! There's a good one I heard about . . ." or "Did you ever hear the one about . . ." or "There's a dandy wee joke . . ."

Some of the best "wee" stories have been told over and over again, and heard over and over again, but listeners still get a kick out of them. "I mind one time," many a Valley lad says, and his nimble wit reaches in to "gaffey" a story stored on the back shelf of his mind. A young lad might have heard a story from an old lad. The new generation interpretation retains the basic punch but puts a new "twist on 'er." "Yuh know how she goes," says the lad. "One lad will kinda stretch 'er a wee bit, add a notch or two or maybe tackle a yarn from a different angle."

Some of the best stories have survived over years of retelling. But no one seems to put this kind of thing on paper too much. Some of these "wee" tales have been slipped into this chapter and given a 'Bedore-Butler-Buttle' twist, for your pleasure.

FAITH WILL MOVE A CAR

One time three nuns ran out of gas as they were driving in their model T Ford along the Upper Opeongo Road, an early Ottawa Valley colonization road.

They walked to the nearest farm house, where, with true Ottawa Valley hospitality, the farmer assured them he could provide some gas for the car.

"But goldang it," he said as he scratched his head, "What in the Sam Hill am I gonna put 'er in?

"Oh, by gol," he grinned, "I know!" He ran upstairs and took the thunder mug from the closet under his bedroom washstand.

"This'll do the job," he grinned as he filled the chamber pot with gas.

The three nuns returned to their car and, as they poured the gas from the thunder mug into the gas tank, along came a Presbyterian Minister. He stopped and gaped at the unusual sight.

"Ladies," he smiled, "I may not be of your church, but I sure do admire your faith!"

UP2

BAD CASE OF THE TWO'S

I mind one time they used to tell about these two old lads up The Valley. They had known each other all their lives and together they had been through a lot, both good and bad. They were rough and tough old lads. They figured you could take them as they were, or let them be. It was up to you.

They would argue between themselves all they wanted but if anyone butted in, they'd both turn on the interloper. What they did was none of anybody else's business.

Well I mind hearin' tell of this time they went to pay their respects at the wake of an old friend. Being a sad occasion, the one old lad blew his nose and sniffled a wee bit.

"You old sucky calf," says his chum, putting on a tough front. "You're cryin'!"

"No I'm not," shot back the other old lad.

"Well then what's that water runnin' out of your eyes for?"

"You old crowbait! If you had any medical knowledge at all you'd be able to see right off I have a bad case of the two's."

"What do you mean, *a bad case of the two's?*" snorted his chum, wrinkling up his nose.

"If you had one brain in your ugly head you'd be able to see in a minute I've had TOO many drinks and my eyes are TOO close to my bladder!"

TRUTHFUL

They tell about an old lad on the Opeongo who was dying. The family sent for the priest to give him Last Rites of the Church. At least, this is the way we heard it.

After he had been blessed, the old lad looked up at the priest with resignation. Then, reaching out for a last ray of hope he said, "Tell me father, do ye think there's really a hell?"

The priest replied, "Well, to be truthful Paddy, I don't know. But, in about ten minutes, *you* will!"

CROOKED LAD

"I mind there was this lad I knew up the Opeongo," says a fellow one time. He was standing on the bridge near the Town Hall in Pembroke, looking down at the water. "This lad would do his mother out of her last dollar. In fact, he'd steal the pennies off a dead man's eyes. I mind one time they used to tell about how when he was diggin' a well, he was so crooked he fell out of it!"

"Upon my soul," says this fellow, "I heard the old lads say that when he died he was so crooked they couldn't straighten him out. They tried, but they finally had to bury him in a daisy churn!"

HEAVY FOG

"I mind one time two lads were fishing at the mouth of the Madawaska River," said Abe Savard. "There was a heavy fog, thick as pea soup!

"Says one lad, 'How far are we from shore?'

"The other lad propped an extension ladder up against the fog and climbed up thirty feet before he could see over it.

" 'About forty-five feet,' he says.

" 'Good,' says the other lad and threw out the anchor. Then he drove a ten-inch spike into the side of the fog.

" 'What's that for?' asked his chum.

" 'To hang the fish on when we catch them.'

"They fished, relaxed and patient. About ten minutes later they heard a big SPLASH!

" 'What's that?' his chum exclaimed excitedly, 'a fish?'

" 'No! No!,' says the lad. 'That's just the anchor hitting the water. It finally got down through the heavy fog!' "

I MUST BE GETTING OLD... I FEEL LIKE I'M ROWING UPHILL!

RAMBLIN' PIG

"I mind one time," a lad recollects, "there was this man who had a ramblin' pig. It used to slip under the fence and eat his neighbor's prize potatoes.

" 'Keep that damn pig outta here or I'll shoot it,' the neighbor warned.

"The pig continued to sneak into the garden.

"Well sir, he just couldn't catch that robber hog in his yard and he wouldn't dare shoot it on the other man's land. However, one day, the pig got stuck in the fence and the neighbor shot it dead as a doornail.

"In court, the case was argued at length — for and against. At times tempers flared but eventually the judge ruled against the man who shot the pig.

" 'Mr. Larone,' ruled the judge, who was known for his good sense of humor, 'I must find you guilty in this case and liable for damages. However, I must say you seem very sincere when you claim you shot the pig in defence of your property.'

"Says Larone, 'Yer Honor dat's true. I shot de pig in de fence of my property, h'an 'e would 'ave been right h'on my property h'if 'e 'adn't got 'ees h'ass caught in de fence!'"

WINDY WOLF

One night at the old Central Hotel in Arnprior Jimmy Connelly was stumped for a story but he didn't let that stop him.

"I mind one time there was an old lad up near Dacre who was turrible afraid of wolves but he really liked to play cards with the lads.

"One night, he got to winning pretty good and didn't notice how late it was getting. Suddenly he jumped up, 'It's gettin' pretty dark out there, lads,' he said excitedly. 'I better be gettin' home.'

"He lit an old lantern figurin' the light and the flame would keep the wolves away, and he took off for home. Ten minutes later he rushed back in through the hotel door. His chums asked him, 'Were the wolves after you, Pat?'

"Breathing hard, white-faced he gasped, 'Wolves? You could hear them up in the Opeongo hills just a-howlin'. I thought I was safe with me old lantern 'til I looked down. There beside me was a grey-nosed old wolf. He had his nose right up to me lantern goin' 'Phooff! Phooff!' — trying to blow me lantern out!' "

TALL PINE

A lad says one time, "You don't have a helluva lot of big buildings around here, do you?"

"No, we don't," says Paddy, "but we've got some great pine trees. One time a chum of mine and me run into a bunch of turrible, monstrous size pine.

"My chum and I laid our cross cut saws and axes on the ground and walked around that tree looking up to see which way would be best to fell it.

"Do you know," says Paddy, "by the time we got all the way around that tree, a foot and a half had rotted off of our axe handles?"

A GREAT PRODUCIN' PINE

"I mind one time," this lad says, "we were helping to take some logs out of a virgin bush. We cut an enormous red pine. She was a turrible great producin' pine. We took fourteen twenty-foot logs out of it," he boasted, "five and a half cord of birch out of the top and ten cedar fence posts from the limbs!"

BIG HAYSTACKS

They used to build some big haystacks on the Opeongo. You could climb up on one at Brudenell and see the lights of Renfrew Town.

"So, what's the point?" a lady asks this old lad.

"Well, ma'am," says he, "you see the town of Renfrew is about a hundred miles from Brudenell, so a haystack had to be high."

"How high?"

"Maybe a hundred feet."

"How can a haystack be a hundred feet high?" the lady queried.

"Well now ma'am I'll tell you." The old lad cleared his throat and squinted his eyes. "You see first of all they built the bottom in an old log barn with the roof off. They pitched hay up for the next round. Then they threw ropes over top of the stack, tied them to the wagons, and used four teams of horses to haul the wagons to the top of the stack. Some lads up there forked them off. Soon it got too high for that.

"A neighbor had a family of pet 'coons who carried up mouthfuls of hay.

"Now she's gettin' pretty high by this time," the old lad continued, a deep frown cutting across his leathery brow. "Young lads were taking up forkfuls on rope ladders. They were up about ninety feet by this time and the boss 'stack builder

says, 'Boys, we gotta put a top on 'er tuh run rain. Now how're we gonna do it?'

"Up steps a wee short man and says, 'Look here! I've got some trained pigeons what will carry straw by straw up there and I'm small enough, I can round off the top and slide back down on a rope! You lads tie ropes onto the rope I take up, and bind down the ends when I put them over the other side.'

"That's how they did it," the old lad smiled. "Yes, ma'am, the tallest haystacks in The Valley are built at Brudenell on the Opeongo!"

BUCKING THE BARLEY

A fellow was cutting a field of barley. It was a terrible good crop and still growin' to beat the band but he had to cut it because the weather was threatenin' early frost.

When he got to the field a big buck was feeding on the grain. Well sir, the lad tied his team of horses to a fence post and hit out, lickity split, through the barley to get his gun.

He found it tough goin', fightin' them big, barley stalks all the way to the house and all the way back. By the time he got back the buck was gone and the snow was a foot deep!

So he cut the barley, but had to leave foot-long stalks sticking out of the ground. Them stalks was so strong, lads snowmobiled clean over top of them all winter.

The next spring, he sawed off the stalks and used them for firewood. One cord of them stalks burned long as ten cord of hard maple!

BUCK SET

"What's a 'Buck Set'?"

The old lad laughed when the young lad asked him. "You mean to say you don't know what a 'Buck Set' is? Well sir, now I'll tell you. You see, in the bush shanty there were no women. When the lads wanted to let off steam on a Saturday night, during the long winter, they would have a square dance.

"A fiddler, a lad with a wee squeeze box, a banjo player, and a fella with a mouth organ, maybe a jews harp or a piece of cigarette paper on a comb, would provide all the music they needed.

"Four couples, or eight men to a set, to form the square dance. Four of the lads would put on aprons to represent women. If they were short one person, then one man would carry a broom and pretend it was his partner.

"The participants were all bucks, no does, hence a *Buck Set!*"

CROSS CUTTING

They used to tell about two neighbor lads on the Opeongo Line. Pat was cross-eyed and Johnny stuttered pretty badly.

"Well sir," Pat says one time to Johnny, "would ye help me kill a beast?"

"Sure," says John, "Tumorruh."

Next day, Johnny came to Pat's place and they got this big steer hog-tied to a gate post.

Johnny says, "Okay, Pat. I'll hold him and you, begub, nail him between the eyes wit' de axe."

So Pat hauls back with the axe, his cross-eyes studyin' where to lambaste the beast.

Johnny started to shake and stuttered, "Fer g-g-gawd's sake, Pat, d-d-d-don't h-h-h-hit where you-re l-l-l-lookin'!"

DRY LAND FROGS

They used to tell about a lad who was working on a piece of land by the road up the Opeongo Line. One day the parish priest happened to drop by for a visit.

"Gidday, Pat, what are ye tryin' to do there?" asks the priest, friendly like.

"Gidday, Father," grins Pat. "Sure I'm makin' meself a hayfield."

"A hayfield?" scoffs the priest. "Sure man, you can't make a hayfield in that field. The land's too wet."

"Oh no, Father. It's not wet atall, atall. It's as dry as a bone. Sure do ye know this land's so dry there's frogs livin' here what are five years old and they can't swim a stroke!"

HOW TO FIGHT A BEAR

One time two lads were hunting on the upper end of White Lake and they put a lad on a runway.

"What'll I do if I meet a bear in the bush," the lad asked.

"My boy," says one of his chums, "do you not know how to fight a bear?"

"No," says he. "How?"

"Well sir," he says, "all you have to do is reach down into the back of your pants, grab a handful of what you find there, throw it into the bear's face — and RUN!"

BOVINE BLOW-UP

"You know," says the old lad to the young lad, "if you watch nature and wild things you can learn a lot.

"I mind this one day, I should have known it was going to be a mortal hot day."

"How come?" the young lad asked.

"Well, you see, I was watching this pond and the steam was rising off it. Some wild ducks flew in and they landed to roost on tree branches, which is strange for ducks. I had a pair of thick-soled boots on so I walked over and felt that pond water. It was real hot!

"That night, the old dog was bringing the cows in from the pasture at milking time and a young heifer darted to one side. The dog snapped at her heels, and when his teeth hit her hoof, they struck a spark and BOOM!!!! The heifer blew up just like a dynamite cap! That was the detonator and that whole herd of cows blew up. You see they had been eating that hot grass all day and that one spark off the dog's teeth set off an explosion.

"Yessir," says the old lad, "that's the first, and only time, I ever saw a whole herd of cattle die of spontaneous combustion!"

SUSPENDED DRINKING

Jack Mooney tended bar many years in The Valley, both during the colorful, old, long bar days and during the less adventurous, more sterile, post-temperance era.

He was an agile, strong man — tall, not broad, but long-muscled in the shoulders. Mooney was quick on his feet and had "guts to burn," even in his sixties when he tended bar in the old Central Hotel.

John, or Jack, we called him both, could see trouble coming one half hour away. He would single out the "shit disturber," take his old pipe out of his mouth, place his hand on the lad's shoulder and say, "Hold on here, Mac. What's goin' on? Drink up your beer and go on ahead home. No arguments, now, or you're on the list and that means you're cut off. Up to you." Most times that was enough to stop a row.

However, if necessary, Jack would get right into it. When he was a young man he was tough. Even as an older man, he wouldn't back down from a fight.

One time two lads went into the bar. One lad put his feet up on a chair.

"Get your feet off that chair," says Jack Mooney. "Did they never teach you any manners at home?"

"Well now that would depend on how you look at it I guess," says one lad as he pulled his feet off the chair. "We've even been known to set our asses on chairs from time to time!"

"PULLIN' A LAD'S LEG"

The Wit of Johnny Coulonge

JOHNNY COULONGE

Johnny Coulonge is a fictional character, a composite of many talespinners I've known, who shows the incomparable Ottawa Valley way of "pullin' a lad's leg" and speaks in the old time Ottawa Valley brogue.

A peaked cap, two or three day crop of grey whiskers, a glint in his eye, and a "Say, just a minute here now 'til I tell you about this lad who . . ." is Johnny Coulonge moving into high gear for swappin' yarns.

Thin, short, wiry, and tough as whalebone. On a long draw, Johnny is always ready to share his full storehouse of humor and wit. It never runs out and Johnny never runs down. Beat him if you can but the odds are against you. You'll have to be head and shoulders above all other talespinners you know if you hope even to hold a candle to Johnny Coulonge while he performs.

Now, Johnny Coulonge is a good lad. Good if he likes you, that is. If he doesn't, well sir then watch out, for he won't give you the time of day. He came through the hungry Thirties. Times were rough. He's alright, old Johnny. He loves to chat and the more he can pull your leg, the better he likes it.

"Them young lads is young buggers sometimes, yuh know," he'll say. "Lazy as a pet coon. Eat yuh out o' house and home and leave yuh lee alone to do the chores sometimes. A body has a turrible time tryin' tuh get anything done around here anymore.

"An' smokin'. That's another thing. If the Lord wanted yuh tuh smoke, he'd a put a chimney on your head!

"By gorrah, them goldang riggons what's flyin' tuh the moon is what a fella should have. Yuh could just hang up there on a cloud and get some peace and quiet once in a while.

"When one things goes wrong, they all go haywire.

"People botherin' me, cows calvin', pigs piggin', all me old hens cluckin' and I have tuh drop everything tuh go hunt an old she-wolf what's tryin' tuh eat me new lambs.

"Turrah tuh hell what the world's comin' tuh.

"Some of them new-fangled rig-a-ma-jigs they're makin' now is good though, yuh know, eh?

"Take them wee grip-ons. They're kinda like pinchers but yuh can squeeze them and they'll hang on, by gawl, 'til the cows come home. They're kinda like pliers like, if yuh know what I mean? Wee grip-ons. Make a damn handy vice, too, fer holdin' a rig tight while yer workin' on it, or fer twistin' off an old rusty nut or bolt what don't want tuh come out the way she went in.

"Oh, I dunno. Kinda makes yuh wonder if she's all worth pluggin' away, but I guess we'll make 'er if the shoe leather hangs out and the ol' lady gets her washin' done.

"Lots o' strangers now, I'm tellin' yuh. I go downtown now and can't hardly meet a face I know. Turrah how the old lads is droppin' off. But I guess them's some of the odds yuh got tuh face if yuh decide tuh hang in."

That's Johnny Coulonge in high gear — and here's more of his playful wit.

MISSUS SIPPY'S RIVER

I recall the time when I first met Johnny Coulonge. I was sitting in one of the old square chairs around the big box stove in Scott's Hardware Store in Pakenham, chatting with Johnny and a few old lads. I was only a youngster of twelve or so and these old lads used to like to tease the young lads a wee bit, when they got the chance.

Says Johnny, "I remember when the Mississippi River only came as far as Carleton Place and stopped right there."

Of course the rest of the old lads agreed, nodding their heads, but, curious, I asked, "How come that happened?"

"Well, now my boy, you see," says he, "we had this fine stone mill here at Pakenham and we even built a nice five-arched stone bridge over the big dip in the rock, in case we ever did get some water to run the mill.

"Times was hard then. To make work the townships hired able-bodied lads and put them to work digging a big ditch from the Ottawa River right up to Carleton Place to join with the river.

"The man's name in charge of that job was Jimmy Sippy. When they made out the bill for that job, his wife signed it, 'Mrs. Jimmy Sippy, paid in full.'

"The County Warden at the next County meeting referred to the bill as 'Missus

Sippy's bill,' and I'll be danged if they haven't called that the 'Missus Sippy River' ever since!

"Over the years, they got to misspelling the river's name and it became known as the 'Mississippi.' But at least we got water for our mill and it made our Five Arch Stone Bridge one of the most famous stone bridges in the world."

DOG WITH GREAT WIND

Deer hunters are never happier than when recounting exceptional accomplishments of the hunt. These stories will stretch as long as is necessary to beat a story someone else has just told. They'll add a couple of prongs to a buck's horns, lay on an extra fifty pounds in weight, and usually swear their shot was at least

250 yards and the deer was on a dead run at the time! Actually, most of the deer they shoot may be at 50 or 60 yards and the deer is standing still, or maybe it was just picking its way along. But that's far too mild. The image of the great hunter must be preserved! And if the hunters run dogs, then *each* one has the best dog.

"You know," Johnny Coulonge says this one time, "a bunch of lads was sittin' around braggin' about how good was their dogs' wind.

" 'My dog can chase four deer, one after another, and hardly puff,' brags one lad.

" 'Never saw my dog pant in his life,' says another.

"I told them," says Johnny, "yuh know it's a terruh how good some of them dogs can be.

"I mind," says he, "I was coming down the lake with a sleigh. About two miles from shore I cut a hole in the ice to water me horses.

"Well sir, my danged old collie dog nosed that wee axe into the watering hole.

"I flung that dog into the watering hole and yelled at him, 'Fetch!'

"The weather was so turrible cold the hole froze over.

"I left, figurin' I had lost me dog. Just before I hit the shore, I cut another waterin' hole. Who climbs outta that hole but that collie dog — with the axe handle in his teeth! Now there's a dog had great wind, I'll tell yuh! Held his breath for *two miles* under the ice in that cold water!"

WISE OLD DOE

"There was once this man named Bob," says Johnny, "who was a great deer hunter. Not being overly fond of mosquitoes, black flies, spiders, deer flies and the like, he didn't venture too often into the great outdoors. However, when fall deer season rolled around, his hunting gang leader would drop him off on the same old point on the north shore of White Lake.

"Bob, big belly and red face, was a jolly old lad. He wore a red and black chequered hunting cap and jacket over heavy underwear, three shirts, and a heavy woollen sweater. On a warm day, he peeled off whatever number of layers left him comfortable.

"His belt invariably slipped down and rolled over under his belly to reveal the white lining of his waistband. To put on his boots over three pairs of socks, two heavy and one light, he had to sit down and pull hard on his foot to get it up close enough to hawk on the boots hard enough to get them on over his heels. Lacing them was a time-consuming chore, one eyelet at a time, then dropping the lace down one side of the boot-top, and reaching under to catch the end so he could pull both ends tight and tie them. After that a few grunts and a heave would get him over on one knee and, catching hold of a tree, he would pull himself to his feet.

"Usually, he faced an opening in the trees and fired at his game from a sitting position, back against a tree. His chums would clean out the deer and throw it in the boat for him. But, by God, there was no way Bob would miss the fall hunt.

" 'Try to stay awake, Bob,' they'd say.

" 'No problem,' Bob would smile as he promptly pulled out a thermos of potent mix from his knapsack, took a few snorts, then leaned back against a big tree to catch up on sleep he lost while hurrying to get to this place. Then he could keep a keen eye open for the much sought after bush beef, commonly known as deer.

"One day, he was sort of snoozin' in the autumn sun when up jumped this big doe heading for the lake.

" 'Well, sir,' Bob later reported to his hunting gang, with a grin, 'she lit out so fast I didn't have time to cock my gun, so I grabbed a rope and threw it over her head. It so happened the rope I grabbed was the one tied to the nose of my boat.

" 'I managed to get a couple of quick shots off but that old doe was throwing waves two feet high! I didn't pluck a hair off her. I hunted and hunted for that boat, but I never did find it!

" 'But you know lads, it's a funny thing. Come the next year I was standin' that same watch and be goldanged if that old doe didn't come swimming down the lake. She was towing the bottom of that old boat and she had two brand new wee fawns on it!' "

OLD MUZZLE LOADER

"My dad made an old muzzle loader one time," Johnny yarned, "and I'm tellin' yuh, she was a dandy. He wouldn't let anyone use her but hisself.

"One time, he was away to town and I figured I'd try 'er out. I put thirteen balls and a wee bag o' gunpowder in my pocket and went huntin' partridge with that old gun.

"Well sir I was lucky and in about two hours I shot thirteen partridge.

"Then I was hurrying home and come across thirteen ducks sitting on a log. I had lotsa powder but I didn't have a single ball to shoot even one danged one of them. But I figured I'd give 'er a try anyways, so I took the ramrod and whittled it sharp on the end and put 'er in the barrel. I took aim and fired 'er. The ramrod went true as an arrow.

"Do you know? I got twelve ducks and if that ramrod had been a few inches longer, I'd have skewered all thirteen of them!"

FISH-TROLLIN' FOOL

"I mind one time in March," says Johnny, "a lad jumped on a big log in some open water at a creek mouth. He rode that log all day, so he did, fishin' off of it.

"Finally he decided to try to spin the log to shore, but it wouldn't spin. It just slowly curved in the middle and moved under the ice leaving him standing in four feet of water.

"His log turned and swam past his leg. He had been trollin' all day off the back of a big pike!"

SCALES

SCALIN' LOGS

One spring, a young lad, fresh from the city, came up and says to Johnny, "I heard some lads who fish up here say the suckers would be runnin' in Fish Creek comin' into White Lake. I just can't believe the stories I heard from those men."

"They've been tellin' you that old story about the spawnin' run. Is that right?"

"Yes," he says. "Is it true?"

"Don't let them pull your leg," says Johnny to the young lad. "Actually the truth is, when the maple sap starts to run the suckers run right down the hills through the trees to the lake. Like any animal, they build up an extra layer of scales durin' the winter and they keep rubbin' off the extra scales on the maple trees."

"I don't believe that," the lad says. "This sounds worse than the stories those other fellas told me!"

"Yuh don't believe that?" says Johnny. "Well, you must have heard about the men who make their living scalin' logs!"

"Yeah," he says.

"Well those slippery scales make it dangerous to chop a tree, so before the loggers can get started they have to send in log-scalers to strip off all those sucker scales to make it safe to use axes and saws.

"Now, if there's anything else you want to get straight and hear the God's honest truth of it, just ask me. Some of these fishermen lads will try to make you believe anything!"

HEAVY FISH RUNS

There used to be some unbelievable heavy spring spawning runs of suckers at the mouth of the Madawaska River where it flows into the Ottawa River at Arnprior.

Says this lad, "One year the run was so heavy, we had to build a plough and sink it so the fish would hit the nose and spread. Then we could get fishing lines down through the suckers and get to where the pickerel were."

"I can believe that," affirms Johnny with a toothless smile and a glint in his eye. "Me and me uncle used to fish there. We'd put ten pound lead sinkers on our lines and those turrible, thick runs of suckers would carry them heavy ten pound sinkers a hundred, maybe two hundred yards up the Madawaska River against the fast current before the sinkers would get to the bottom!"

SUBMARINE SNOWMOBILE

"One time," says Johnny, "this lad was trailin' a rope with a minney pail tied to it, kinda trollin' like, hopin' one o' them big gar pike with the saw on his snout would saw through the ice to get one o' them minneys and he'd have himself a fish. He got careless and his snowmobile sank through some thin ice. He saw it comin', jumped off, and ran for shore.

"Just as he got to land, his old snowmobile came nosin' up out of the ice at the water's edge. It climbed up the bank, spluttered, and stopped. Yuh know, she has to be the best old snowmobile on the lake. He dried off the plugs, pulled the startin' cord, and she purred like a kitten. Soon he was sittin' warm and snug by his old cook stove eatin' the smelts he had bought for bait that day!"

SQUEAKS AT $5.00 EACH

Johnny was a good man in the bush. He could turn his hand to anything. He made his own axe handles and ground his axes on an old hand grind stone. The grind stone had handles on the side and the wheel turned through water in a kind of small water trough on legs.

Johnny always filed his own hand saws, swede saws, and big cross-cut saws.

Johnny was telling the lads about a joke he pulled on a young greenhorn who was up in the bush for the first time and was pretty gullible.

"He didn't know nothing about nothing, if you know what I mean," says Johnny.

"One day I says to this young lad, 'Do you hear the squeaks when I file this saw?'

" 'Yep,' he says.

"Well tell your boss I want him to send me a good, solid, nail keg to ketch them squeaks in. I can sell 'em for five dollars a piece in any music shop," says Johnny.

"His boss fell in with the joke and sent him back with a nail keg and a note that said, 'The only thing I didn't do was bore a hole in the lid so you could get the squeaks into the barrel.' "

SWITCHIN' FOR WATER

"I mind the coldest year I ever seen," says Johnny, "was the year the freeze-up came in July. The next mornin' a flock of wild ducks flew away from behind our place with a wee lake froze to their feet. They flew clean to Chicago where all that ice melted and caused a turrible flood on the Mississippi River.

"Talkin' about floods, yuh know we've had some danged dry years, too, when there was hardly no water at all. I mind one dry year there was scarcely a well in the country that wasn't dry.

"I was sittin' at the mouth of Sucker Crik thinkin' about all the great sucker runs there used to be. All of a sudden I hear this turrible clatter comin' down the dry rocks on the falls and here is this old beaver, with a stick in his mouth switchin' for water."

SOME ARCHEOLOGY HISTORY

There was a bunch of lads one time swappin' yarns with Johnny Coulonge in the corner store at White Lake.

"I mind one time," says this old lad, Jack, "Sandy McGregor, the blacksmith, made a fish hook for me from a prong of one of them old iron hay rakes. I tied it on a chunk of clothes line I bought at Freddie Ostler's store and baited it with a skinned groundhog.

"I started to troll around in my canoe.

"Ten feet off shore, I got a nibble but nothing to hold.

"Then I got a dandy bite, set the hook, and held on. I had hold of a big pike. He took me on the merriest ride I ever had. Five trips we made around White Lake before that fish got tired. I'll be goldanged though, I could not pull him out of the water! I had to tie him to a tree and go get Billy Box to come with his team of horses.

"Billy Box was a small, quiet man. He always greeted folks with a pleasant, warm smile and a firm handshake. He impressed 'em as a steady worker who lived in a wee, neat house on the road to White Lake, just past Ostlers' Store.

"Billy got him out alright, but he had to add five feet to the wagon reach to keep it from dragging on the ground.

"Everybody in White Lake got a snack of that giant pike before I buried the bones up in Watty Hanson's gravel pit. Now I hear about them archeology history lads findin' whale bones up around there. Yuh know those whale bones is really nothing but ribs from that giant pike I caught and buried in Watty's Pit!"

ONLY 10 MORE
CHOPPING DAYS
'TIL CHRISTMAS
Ft.
0
1
2
3
4
5
6

STRETCHIN' IT A BIT

"Yuh know," says Johnny, "one time I explained cross cut sawin' tuh two young, Quebec City, French lads I worked with in Carp.

" 'Well, sir,' says I, 'look here now. I know you lads are dang good workers. Maybe I could get you a job workin' in the bush for the winter.'

" 'What would we be doing?'

" 'Fellin' trees,' says I.

" 'They give you a five and a half foot cross cut saw when you go into the bush in the fall and they expect you to work it so hard it'll heat up and stretch. They want it stretched to six feet by Christmas time. That way they know you've been working, not just putting in time.'

"I told them I did it myself when I worked in the bush.

"They went back to Quebec. Two months later, a big, burly lad came on our job.

"Says he, 'Say, did you tell a couple o' young lads you could work a cross cut saw so hard it would get red hot and stretch from five and a half feet to six feet between fall and Christmas?'

" 'Well now,' I says, 'I might have.'

" 'Well those young lads have told everybody from Montreal to the Gaspé about a lad, name of Johnny Coulonge, in the Ottawa Valley, what can pull a cross cut saw so fast the pull of the pine gum will stretch it. Turrah how a good true story'll get turned into a lie, ain't it?' "

LET THE CHIPS FALL

"I was walkin' up John Street one morning with an axe and a swede saw on my back and a pack sack made out of a potato sack tied at both ends with some binder twine," says Johnny. "We called it a *Turkey*."

"I met the two Arnprior policemen, and the chief asked me what I was intendin' to do with the saw and the axe.

" 'I'm going' to cut some wood,' says I.

" 'Well,' says he, 'chop all the wood you want, but clean up your mess. I don't want to see any of your woodchips flying into the streets and cluttering up the town.'

"Well sir now I was choppin' wood near White Lake, about ten miles south of Arnprior, and though I tried my best, do you know when I got back to town here's the two policemen with two tin pails picking up hardwood chips on the outskirts of Arnprior!

"I guess when I got to really workin' hard I forgot meself and really made them chips fly!"

> 63

"HOLDIN' FORTH"

The Adventures of Dinny O'Brien

PREFACE

A nasal twang and a tall black hat on a spare frame of medium height made up the high points of a man who could come back with a witty answer quicker than any man I ever knew. I met Dinny O'Brien and talked with him in the old Central Hotel in Arnprior when I was only a lad of thirteen years. Dinny would "hold forth" around a table, philosophizing, arguing, spouting his opinions, and loudly disagreeing whenever and with whomever he fancied.

Dinny was one of a kind, crusty, witty, canny, with no particular desire to work long and hard for himself but he was always ready to help anyone else. Still, Dinny was a man not to tangle with in a duel of words. Second best was the most anyone could expect to get out of it.

Stories of Dinny O'Brien's wit and humor are told time and again across the Almonte-Corkery country, and further afield west to Ottawa. Some of the best Dinny stories I've heard were told to me by Mickey Joe Flynn who was bent over with rheumatism when I first met him. A burly old lad with a shock of white hair and a sort of unique high voice, he always had a half smile glowing on his face that matched his bright sense of humor. Mickey Joe was a second hand dealer, and the yard behind his wee house was filled with everything from soup to nuts, as they say.

I taped Mickey Joe one time, telling stories about Dinny O'Brien, and for years after he would drop into my house in Arnprior, sometimes with his brother, "Dinnis." "Bernard," he'd say, "would yuh play that tape for me?"

Mickey Joe Flynn told of the time he was crossing a pasture with Dinny. They came to a wee creek and had to step from stone to stone to cross it. Making his way over, Mick fell in the water. Slightly embarrassed, he crawled out onto the creek bank.

"Mind yuh," says Mick, "I'm usually quick on my feet. I just kinda slipped by accident. I could walk a tightrope, so I could."

"Walk a rope?" snorts Dinny. "Why man, you can scarcely walk the ground!"

Dinny O'Brien's adventures have become legends, part of the rich folklore of the Ottawa Valley. Here are a few exploits of this opinionated, stubborn, and wonderfully humorous Ottawa Valley Irishman who haled from the Burnt Lands of Huntley near Almonte.

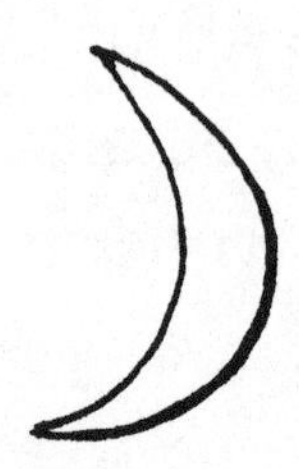

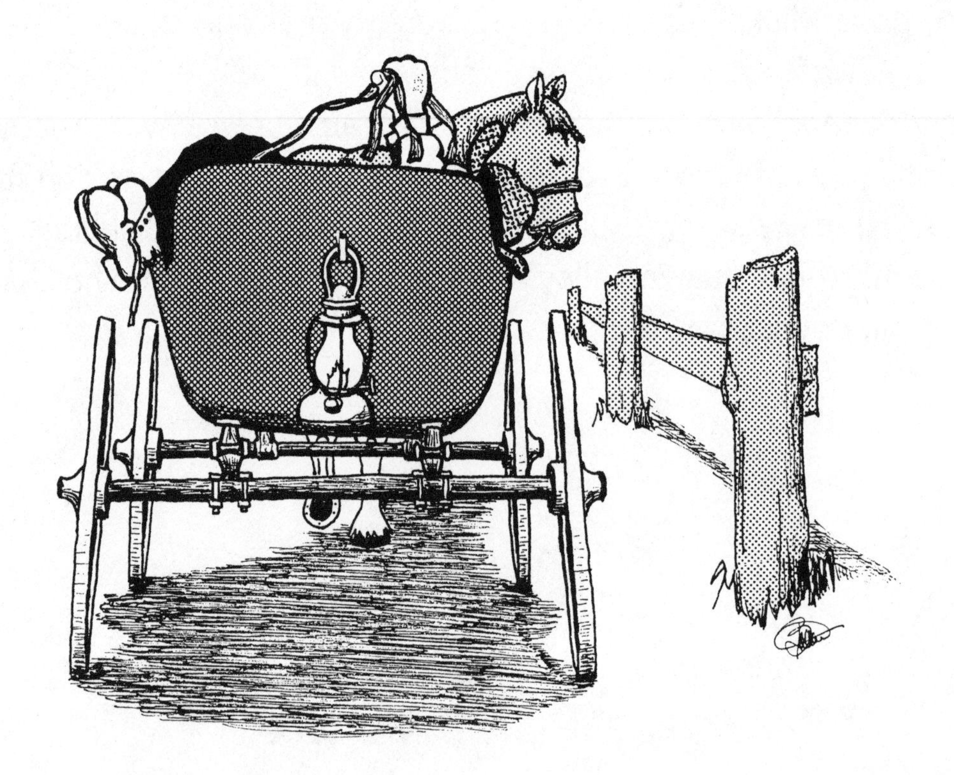

SAFE HOME

During the hungry Thirties, Dinny O'Brien would ride into Arnprior from Almonte to sit with the old lads gathered at the Central Hotel.

"Gidday," Dinny would say to me in his nasal twang, as he tied his old horse in the shed. "See this lad gets some oats and a wee lock of hay fer dinner time and supper time." He always made sure someone would take care of his old horse while he was in town.

"And be damn sure ye water him. I'll check his snout fer dewdrops," he warned.

The bar in those lean years was open from eight o'clock in the morning until midnight. Dinny would arrive at opening time and leave shortly before closing. He'd wave to his chums and yell, "Gidday to yez all!"

They would laugh in return, "Safe home, Dinny!"

"Do yuh think he can find his way home?" one would ask.

"No," another would answer, "but his horse can!"

LOST LANDS

Dinny didn't do as much around his own farm as he might have. They used to say he was better outside his fence than inside it. If a lad needed a hand, Dinny was ready to jump in and help, always "Johnny-on-the-spot."

A drinking man, he had a weakness for the creature, old Johnny Barleycorn. That, and his easy come, easy go approach to life, reduced his land from three farms to one.

One day, Dinny was sitting in the dentist's chair in Arnprior. The dentist was kind of looking into Dinny's open mouth. His head back, Dinny talked in his slow drawl around the dentist's mirror and probe.

"Do yuh see anything down there, Doc?"

"No, Mr. O'Brien," answers the dentist, quite seriously, "I don't."

"Well sir, bejabers yuh should," snorted Dinny. "Swallow by swallow, there's two farms down there!"

DENNIS AND JESUS

They tell about the time a new priest was visiting his parishioners. Dinny was puttering around his front yard when the priest came to see him.

"Gidday, Father," says Dinny.

"Good afternoon! Would you be Dinny O'Brien?"

"Dennis, Father!" Dinny replied, "Dennis O'Brien!"

"And how old would you be, Dennis?"

"Thirty-three. Same year as our Lord when he departed from this world. In material possessions, we're about the same. For good deeds, He has me beat!"

WASTE NOT — WANT NOT

Dinny was visiting with old friends in the hotel bar this one morning. They sampled big quarts of cold ale fairly generously. The day crept around to dinner time. One of Dinny's chums asked, "Are you ready to come on in to dinner, Dennis?"

"Come on in to dinner?" Dinny snorts. "Are you nuts? No sirree! Not yet! These are hard times and a man can't afford to be wasteful. Waste not. Want not. Be damned if I'm gonna spoil a ten dollar glow with a fifty cent meal!"

DRUNK AGAIN

One night, as Dinny came out of the Almonte Hotel, he bumped smack into the parish priest.

"Well!" says the priest, "drunk again!"

"Don't let it bother yuh at all, at all, Father," grins Dinny. "Yuh don't look too bad. I often get that way meself."

CONDEMNED TO HELL

One time in the bar of the old Central Hotel, a salesman called Dinny "an old billygoat." That started a small argument. Although they shook hands, Dinny didn't forget it.

That evening men from the bar came into the dining room. I was waiting on tables. "What'll you gentlemen have?" I asked them generally. Because it was the Lenten season, I knew Roman Catholics and Anglicans would order eggs or fish.

"What'll you have, Mr. Connelly?" I asked my old lumberman friend, Jimmy.

"Eggs, please," answered Jimmy, always a fine old gentleman.

"And you, Mr. O'Brien?" I asked Dinny.

"Aigs," growled Dinny as he separated his knife and fork a bit more on the table, readying himself to go right at it as soon as the plate appeared.

Said the salesman, "I'll have pork chops."

Dinny whirled on him, roaring, "Say! ! ! !"

"Yeh?" questioned the startled salesman.

"Do yuh eat meat a-Friduh?"

"Of course I do," retorted the salesman.

"Ah suh bejabers," snorted Dinny. "When yuh die, they'll strap a piece of fat pork on yer ass and yuh'll slide right into hell!"

FORTY BELOW

Old Valley hotels usually had only a box stove or two and a kitchen cook stove to supply heat during the winter. Upstairs the bedrooms would get "turrible" cold, as the lads would say. One stormy winter night, Dinny slept in the Almonte Hotel. The next morning was frosty. He came downstairs and stood bent over with his backside close to the old box stove. As he rubbed the heat into his legs with his hands, he exclaimed, "Boyso! Must be forty below and droppin'!"

A lad from one of the townships had come into town early with a sleigh load of wood. He dropped into the hotel to warm up a bit. As he approached the stove, Dinny looked at the white frost on the old lad's eyebrows. Icicles had frozen on his moustache and beard where his breath had frosted. Dinny growled, "Hah! Bejabers, me old bucko, you look even colder than me. What room did they have you in last night?"

THE IMPOSTER

One night, Dinny was riding down the main street of Almonte in his buggy. His old horse trotted right along.

He came to the new O'Brien Theatre, one of a chain which had been established at the time in many towns of the Ottawa Valley. It stood there in all its new glory, lights blazing out in the night.

His young lad was sitting straight up, all bug-eyed beside him. Dinny turned to him and said, "Yuh know, son, you never can tell what O'Brien owns."

He pointed to the new theatre. "Look, there! You see?" says Dinny, "O'Brien in lights!"

WARTIME LEVELLIN' BOARD

During the Second World War, the Canadian government established a Wartime Prices and Trade Board. It was a special government service with inspectors who traveled throughout Canada enforcing regulations governing the prices that could be placed on goods, materials, machinery, and other products. If it had not been in place, greedy people would have squeezed the last cent out of folks for goods that were "hard to come by."

Many things had to be rationed during the Second World War because they were in "survival production." All effort was concentrated on producing those things required to support the war effort. Dinny thought it was a dandy rig and a smart move. He found it exceptionally fine because it kept farm suppliers from charging too much.

"It sort of levels things out," said Dinny, "if you know how to work it." He made sure all rules were observed when he was buying goods from people who had control over prices. Selling, now that was another thing. Dinny figured it was alright for him to set his own prices with an understood little bit "to boot" for personal services. Any extra would go in the sock and no need for it to show up on records. Actually, according to many lads' way of thinking, there were things that were nobody's business but their own. The old lads didn't like to be told what to do and had a hard time following rules. After all, the big shots had more money than they did so why not steer the system in their favor?

Just imagine Dinny, with a sly grin, singing,

"We thank the Lord
for many a thing.
For the Levellin' Board,
we thank Mackenzie King!"

DYIN' GOOD

Dinny was seventy-five years old when he died.

They say there were three people standing by his death bed. Dinny opened his eyes, looked them over, and muttered, "It looks like I'm dyin' good. I guess this may be the only time I'll beat the Lord. As I remember it, he had only *two* thieves beside him when he died — and I've got *three!*' "

ME PENANCE

Dinny met the parish priest one day on Almonte's main street. The good Father asked, "Will I be seeing you at confession soon, Mr. O'Brien?"

"Confession, Father?" exclaims Dinny. " 'Pon me soul, I don't think I could come good for any more sins. I'm still catchin' up on me penance since the last time I was in the box!"

AUTHORITY ON THE BIBLE

On a rainy day farmers often take the opportunity to come into town. It's too wet to work at the hay anyway.

So, this one time Dinny was chatting with a few of them in Hickey's Blacksmith Shop in Almonte. Says one lad, "What do you think of the donations they're asking for the buildin' of the new church?"

One old lad speaks up, "Well sir, now I'll tell yuh, I don't have a lot of ready cash, so I'm gonna donate a beast." Another lad says, "That's a good idea! All of us farmers should do that."

Dinny whirled on the "would be organizer of good deeds" with a scornful, withering scowl. "All of us should do *what?*"

"We should give a steer to go towards raising funds."

"Give away a good steer we been feedin' all winter! And why should we do *that?*" growls Dinny.

"Well, Dennis, afterall," says the lad, "it's all done in the name of the Lord. It's only right we do our part."

"Well sir now I figure there's sense and reason in most things, but I see neither in this idea," mutters Dinny.

"How come?" they all asked.

Says Dinny, "If you're all as Christian as you're trying to make out to be, you should know your Bible. I'll admit there's mention in there He often had to do with sheep and goats. But I'll be danged if I can recall He was ever in the cattle business!"

THINK SHE'LL BE A BIT HIGH-STRUNG ?
NOT IF YOU DON'T FIDDLE WITH HER!
SHEESH! I THINK I'LL RUN AWAY AND JOIN EWEY LEWIS AND THE EWES!

DO-RE-MI-EWE

Dinny kept a few sheep. He clipped a bit of wool, traded, got a few lambs every year, and had an odd snack of mutton.

One time an old ewe had a hard time delivering a lamb. Dinny called the vet to help her in the birthing. She was a small beast and afterward the vet had to sew her up. He asked Dinny if he had any thread.

"No, I don't have nothin' at all," says Dinny, "but wait just a minute now. Hold onto yer horses and I'll fix yuh up."

He went in to the farmhouse and took one of the cat gut strings off an old fiddle. The fiddle string worked just dandy. When the vet finished his suturing job, Dinny cut the old ewe loose and gave her a slap on the rump.

As she scampered away, Dinny yelled, "There now, DO-RE-MI! Yuh'll have music in yer rear end the rest of yer life!"

MERRY-GO-ROUND

One time Dinny and his wife, Mary, were at the Almonte Fair. A trip into town was always a good excuse for Dinny to put a few drinks under his belt. When Dinny got to boozin', he got cantankerous and you never knew what he would do. After a few trips to the Hotel, Dinny got to feeling pretty good and he and Mary decided to take a wee joy ride on the Merry-go-round.

Dinny liked the ride and the music so well he wouldn't get off and made up a song about it right there and then. He had such a great, powerful voice you could hear him singing all over Almonte.

Dinny just said, "Let 'er rip!" hung on and sang his Merry-Go-Round Song 'til he was "danged good and ready to get off!"

> "Dinny and Mary went into town
> and Dinny got onto the Merry-go-round.
> Dinny said he would not pay.
> Oh ee yay, ai yee, hi yay!"

PADDLE YOUR OWN CANOE

When Dinny's lease was up on the farm, he didn't want to leave it.

The case ended up in court and the judge refused Dinny's plea, declaring that Dinny had to make good on the mortgage — pay his debt or give up the farm.

Dinny was pretty down-hearted. "But what about me son?" says Dinny. "What'll he do, yer Honor?"

"Let him paddle his own canoe," says the judge.

"And who," inquired Dinny, with his best sly-eyed smile, "who, yer Honor, is goin' out on a limb to buy and present this canoe to him?"

SALESMAN-ITIS

One evening a farm machinery salesman made his way towards Dinny with the glad hand out. "Good evening, Mr. O'Brien," says the salesman flashing a big, friendly smile.

Dinny didn't like salesmen. However, he stopped and set down the pail of milk he was carrying to the house from the cow byre.

"Gidday," says Dinny. He figured he couldn't be just downright ignorant. He hitched a boot up on a wagon wheel hub, all the while trying to figure out how to get rid of the salesman.

Well sir, fate smiled on Dinny that day. Along came the old dog, cocked his leg up and let 'er fly into the milk. "Get out of there, yuh brute, yuh!" Dinny roared. "Now before I can give this man some milk to take home I'll have to strain 'er all over again." Then, he looked the salesman square in the eye and asked in a neighborly kind of way, "Say! Would yuh like tuh stay fer supper?"

The salesman gulped, swallowed quickly, then turned a sickly green. He thanked Dinny, "Maybe some other time, Mr. O'Brien," and turned smartly. His heels kicked up dust as he headed for the gate.

Dinny chuckled, "I'll have to feed this milk to the pigs but it's worth it to get rid of that nosy peddler!"

INNOCENT 'TIL PROVED GUILTY

Dinny could always come back with a sharp answer. One time he argued his own case in front of a judge. There was every reason to believe Dinny should not have won, but he did.

The judge pointed his cane at Dinny. "Mr. O'Brien! I can't help but think there is a guilty man at the end of this cane."

"Yes, yer Honor," drawled Dinny, "but I wonder which end of the cane the guilty one is on."

"STRETCHIN' THE TRUTH"

The Reminiscences of Paddy Garvey
and his son, the Bard of the Bonnechere

PREFACE

Paddy Garvey was a man who brought the wit and humor of the true old Irishman to the Ottawa Valley of Canada. A short, sturdy, broad-shouldered, hardworking pioneer of the upper Bonnechere country, Paddy's mind would smile on the world. No one ever heard a bad word spoken about him, only that he made the best of a life which was both difficult and beautiful. I can still picture him in my imagination with a smile and a twinkle in his observant eyes as they crinkle around the corners.

Paddy came into the headwater country of the Bonnechere River early in his lifetime. He named his settlement "Sligo" after his home in Ireland. When the Ontario government marked off the boundaries of Algonquin Park they took in Paddy's land — simply kicking him out. It hurt Paddy deeply to have to leave his old home. He fought it as hard as he could, but there was no way he could beat the government. So he moved to make his home in the Village of Killaloe.

Paddy liked to reminisce. Being an old Irish Valley lad, he wasn't above stretchin' the truth a bit. Of course he talked in the colorful old Valley Irish tongue.

"I mind," Paddy used to say, with a twinkle in his eye, "one time I went tuh 'Terawntuh' tuh meet one o' them guvermint lads. We were up on the tenth floor of the Ryall Yark Hotel, down near the big lake, yuh know.

“Well sir, now we got tuh arguing, me and this guvermint lad. Pretty soon things got hot and heavy and we got into ’er hammer and tongs.

“We started tuh rassle and roll around the floor and begad we fell out the windah, all the way tuh the ground — from the tenth floor!

“But never mind,” says Pat, “I had the bastard licked before we hit the ground!”

I also knew Paddy’s son, Martin. Martin was a cut off the old stick. He didn’t have the physical strength or the “off the top” Irish wit Paddy brought from Ireland, but he had another fine attribute. Martin was a poet of note. People from far and wide across The Valley knew Martin as the “Bard of the Bonnechere.”

Martin lived in Paddy’s big white house in Killaloe. He called it the “White House on Washington Square” because an old lad named Washington once lived there, in a wee shanty.

Before Martin went any place he would insist on stopping at “The Fountain.” “We’ll get two mickeys of poteen,” he’d say, “just in case we only need one.”

“Why in tarnation don’t you put the electric in, Martin?” a lad asked him.

Martin smiled and answered in his famous poetic fashion,

“Oh no! No! No!
That way I will not go
for sure as McGinty had a goat
the coal oil’s good for my throat!”

TURRIBLE BIG JUMP

It was hunting time in The Valley and a bunch of the lads were in Finnucan's kitchen, in Killaloe, sitting around the table telling about past achievements, big bucks, hard runs through swamps, sly old deer, good dogs, and great deer country.

The fall deer hunt in The Ottawa Valley is one of the year's highlights.

"I mind one time," says Paddy, "now that yuh bring it tuh mind with some of them yarns about the hunting days. I mind I was huntin' at Sligo on the Upper Bonnechere River this early mornin' in November and sirree begad I hits this monstrous big buck with a spread from point tuh point like a bull moose.

"I nailed him at about fifty yards. She was a straight shot from a wee knoll across a beaver meadow.

"Now I knew I hit him, but be damned he took tuh runnin' like the wind. There was no way I could let him get away so I took right after him 'cross country.

"He ran down the Bonnechere, past Killaloe, but I'm right on his tail. He passed Golden Lake and kept going on out towards Dacre where he jumped the Constan Crik and begad I jumped 'er right after him."

"My goodness, Mr. Garvey," said the woman of the house where the hunters had gathered, "that must've been a turrible big jump!"

"T'was so, Mrs. Finnucan," says Paddy, "t'was so! But yuh'll have tuh mind I had a fifty-mile run at 'er!"

> 99

TURRIBLE HEAVY

Paddy had been helpin' out a neighbor this one time and when it came supper time the woman of the house asked him to stay and have a bite to eat with them. Paddy was "batchin' it" at the time. His wife was away for a few days so he was glad to get a home-cooked meal.

Well they got to talking and trading yarns around the supper table and of course Paddy was never stuck for a story to tell. They were sipping their green tea after their dessert and Paddy says, "Yuh know one time I walked tuh Renfruh tuh buy one of them fannin' mill rigs.

"The lads at the hardware store helped me to strap 'er on me back and I headed fer Killaloe.

"When I got tuh Eganville I bought a sow pig. She was goin' fer a good price and I couldn't pass up the deal. I tied a rope 'round her neck and she led good.

"Everything was goin' great until just when we got to Golden Lake that old sow had a litter of wee pigs."

The little old grandmother of the house was listening intently to Paddy's story and feeling sorry for him. "My, Mr. Garvey, bringin' that big fannin' mill, all the way from Renfrew on your back. That must have been a turrible heavy carry!"

"T'was so a heavy carry, Ma'am," grinned Paddy. "But yuh know, the worst part of it was runnin' around through the bush with that big fannin' mill on me back trying to catch them danged, squealin' little pigs!"

TOO MUCH BOTHER

Paddy was a stocky lad, short, but wide-shouldered and strong. Sometimes, he used to carry bags of grain on his shoulders to Renfrew, and then carry the ground flour back to Killaloe.

He'd often meet one of his chums coming down the road with a horse and wagon and of course he'd never go by a lad without stopping to pass the time of day.

Paddy would hitch his foot up on the wagon wheel hub and light his old pipe. They'd smoke and chat and maybe be there for fifteen minutes, a half hour, or more but Pat wouldn't even bother to take the 100-pound bag of flour off his shoulder.

"Too much bother to pick it up again," he'd say.

I NEED ME FEED

"I mind one time," Paddy was telling these lads, "the wife and I walked from Killaloe to Eganville to buy a brand new cook stove.

"I carried that stove on me back. She was fairly heavy, but when I got to Golden Lake I just built a raft and headed up the lake to Killaloe.

"The stove acted kind of like a sail picking up the wind, so we sat back and relaxed.

"Bejabers," says Paddy, "buildin' that old raft made me turrible hungry. To keep up me strength, like any old horse, I needed me feed.

"So I rigged up a fishin' line, took a red feather from me wife's hat, and wired it to a hook. Before long I had a couple of bass caught and cleaned fer the fryin' pan.

"I lit a dandy fire in the stove. The wife soon had a great wee snack of fish boilin' to beat the band as we were steamin' up Golden Lake with the black smoke pourin' outta the stack.

"Yuh know," grinned Paddy, "a fella's got tuh look after his health and, as the lad says, 'The Lord helps them as helps themselves.' "

ONE TONGUE BETWEEN US

Paddy was enjoying a quart with a bunch of lads in the settin' room of the Killaloe Hotel one afternoon, when a wedding party passed by. The horses and buggies were all decked out for fair.

"There's another poor lad's got shafted," grunted an old bachelor from where he sat, in a broad captain's chair, by the window.

"How do you make that out?" asked Paddy.

"When the bride's got the weddin' horse harnessed between the shafts, she's got the lad where he can't back down. He's shafted!" the bachelor snorted back.

"Yup," grinned another, "even the weddin' horse is dressed in black — mournin' for the poor lad!"

"Well sir, for me," laughed Paddy, "you can't say I got shafted. You know me. When I see something I want, nobody's gonna stop me, come hell or high water. I can't say I swept me bride off her feet, but I sure pulled her right out of the water, in a way of speakin'.

"I was driving stagecoach into the Upper Bonnechere Country, to Sligo one time," continued Paddy, "on my way to a Stopping Place up in the area now called Algonquin Park. When I saw this beautiful young woman get aboard at Killaloe, I decided then and there, 'She's fer me!'

"The spring flood was high and I knew the old bridge across the Bonnechere River couldn't take the weight of both horses and stage at one time. So, I unhitched the horses and tied a long rope to them. Then I led them to the shore,

downside of the bridge, by the water. Leaving them there, I walked across the bridge, carrying the end of the rope. From the other side of the river, I pulled both horses into the water. The current caught them and they swam like hell while I pulled on about 3600 pounds of horses! They swung down river a wee bit but I landed them and led them to the end of the bridge. Then I walked over and picked up the tongue of the stagecoach. She was stuck in the mud so I started rockin' 'er to get 'er started. But gol' danged if that fine, good lookin' woman didn't get out of the coach to lend a hand!

" 'Come on,' she said, 'let's pull together.' We managed to pull that stage over the bridge across the Bonnechere River! That's how I met me bride!" Pat grinned proudly.

"Her name was Josephine Augusta Precufski. She'd come to the Bonnechere to work for Dennis McGuey. He and his wife, the former Margaret Foy, ran the Stopping Place eight miles above Basin Depot.

"We got married soon after, in the year 1885, and we've been pullin' together ever since, so to speak. You know, in all the years we've been married we've never fought or wrangled."

"How come?" one old bachelor asked skeptically.

"Well," says Pat, "I figure it's because we started out with just one tongue between us — and I was smart enough to leave 'er that way!"

POETIC HISTORY

Martin Garvey would take anyone who was interested on a trip from Sligo, Paddy's old home on the Upper Bonnechere, down to Traymore at the head of Golden Lake near Killaloe.

He would stand on the river shore, dip some water into his glass, mix in some poteen, raise it up to the hills of Ben Bulben, and say,

> "We'll take the sweet water
> at the Bonnechere shore
> and drink a toast
> as we've done before!"

He'd show the small pole-enclosed cemetery where a whole family was buried, and tell of the dreadful smallpox epidemic.

He'd point out Mother Squaw Rock: "The Indians say river

drivers raped a young woman there and ever since, when the moon is high during the spring flood, people passing on the river can hear her cry out in terror."

Martin recorded history in poem and sometimes, fascinated by the magic of the "singing words" flowing off his tongue, he would talk in poetry. As the "song of his Irish soul" warmed to the touch of a jolt of his favorite brew, the Bard would smile that big warm smile of his and whisper, almost sigh, "That's puttin' 'er in there pretty hard, isn't it? — and there's no man other than me can do it, now is there?"

He was right because Sligo was his father's home and no other Bard in The Valley land has the verse in his voice as had Martin Garvey of Killaloe.

Martin once said to me,

"Sligo so cold and so lonely,
Sleeping as cold as a stone
Still Sligo will be glad and quite comely
When Sligo comes back to its own."

But sadly, Sligo never will.

THE BARD HOLDS FORTH

We should mention some of the songs and verse enjoyed one night when The Bard of the Bonnechere held forth in Arnprior on James Street at Doug Scheel's. Doug was ensconced in royal comfort in the best chair in house. Mac Beattie, famous Ottawa Valley tune smith and musician, was urged on by Doug, "Come on now, Mac. You know these people up The Valley, what do you think? Are The Valley characters disappearing like they say?"

"Doug, you have the big chair," interjected The Bard. "You tell us. Since you have the best chair in the house, we'll make you the chairman!"

"No. No. Now you know what I mean, Mac. I mean what do you think?" says Doug with no intention of letting anyone throw him off the track.

Says Mac, as he appraised the crew assembled, "Well, sir, there are still plenty of characters in The Valley, but it's a long time since I've seen so many assembled in one room."

"Oh yes! Oh yes!" smiled The Bard as he sipped generously from his cup of cheer. "To the Shanty we will go brave boys. To the Shanty we will go."

"Come on Martin, sing us a song," chuckles Big Biggs Jack from across the room.

"Oh yes! Oh yes!" quoth the Bard. "Mr. Jack, from Arnprior. So you didn't have anything to do with Jack's Chute on the Bonnechere. And you, the real McKay — wee Jock McKay, the apple of me eye," he directed to Neil McKay.

Eddy Allen says, "Sing The Girl I Left in Brudenell, Martin," and Don Hutt smiled in silent wonder at the Valley Crew assembled there that night.

"It's the Civil War where the guns they roar,
Where the Shot and shell may blind me
Still I'll brace each shell for Brudenell
And the girl I left behind me."

"No, no," urged Helen Scheel. "I want the one about Jim Culhane."

"And so do I, and so do I, says Mac Beattie. So Martin sang, "The Days on the Carcajou."

"I changed that a bit to 'Karka Jour," he mentioned, "because it suits me better. I have a poet's license, you understand," grinned The Bard from Killaloe.

He winked and sang of the gang of the foreman Jim Culhane:

"From Killaloe went many a crew
Along the Bonnechere Road,
With cheer and song they drove along
On their way to that new abode
Of every crew there were some you knew
Still others would say 'Bon Jour'

For there's many a name for Jim Culhane
Went on the Karka Jour."

"Sing a drive song, Martin," someone asked. "Do you know one?"

"Do I know one? Now if *I* don't, now what man would, I ask you?" he grinned and rolled into:

"There were men alive who were on that drive
It's records ne'er been beat
For a million pine they drove that time
With Tom Reynolds on the sweep.
Now on the river those men were clever
Fellows in their prime
On the logs you'd admire going down to Arnprior
The finest of red and white pine.
Boland Bill remembers still
It was eighteen eighty-five
He was one of the few who saw that crew
That weren't afraid to die
For old Sorel through the gates of hell
To drive the Robitaille."

"TRACIN' PEDIGREES"

The Sooth Sayings of Willard

PREFACE

Willard is one Ottawa Valley character whose wit has given me many a chuckle during the years. He is a happy, good natured, friendly lad. I have a great deal of admiration for Willard, for he's been good medicine for me many's the time when I've been down in the dumps.

It takes Willard an hour or more to walk through the Arnprior Mall because everybody is ready to shake hands with him and hear the "news of the day." You can depend on his having the latest word on who is in the "wake house," the result of the most recent trial, roads under construction, the weather forecast, and just about anything else you might want to know.

"Yes! Yes!" Willard will say. "Isn't it a turrah the things that's goin' on!" His bright eyes, set in rosy, chubby cheeks shine and he chuckles as he trades stories. Without doubt, one of the friendliest lads I have ever known and never too busy to pass the time of day.

Willard is also known for his "whistling" good memory. He forgets very little, including names, dates, times, and faces. I will meet him and he'll say, "Bernard Vance Bedore, born March 3, 1923, lived in Renfrew at the British Hotel then moved to Arnprior and lived in the old Central Hotel. Your mother is Catherine, father, Delorme.

FAMILY TREE

"Would that be pretty close, now?"

"Right on, Willard!" I laugh.

"Yes! Yes!" Willard chuckles.

There are few families Willard can't trace back to the great-grandparents on both sides and sometimes even further! He seldom fails to pull names right out of his head.

Says Willard, "Yes! Yes! It's a good thing to know a man's pedigree. Sometimes it helps a person to decide if he should deal with him, or if he shouldn't."

Willard is a great soothsayer who seldom fails to show the true character of the Ottawa Valley as he spins his yarns.

THE INCREDIBLE
Dr. Ray
Sees All
Knows All

DOCTOR RAY

I learned about Doctor Ray one time when Willard and I were telling lies and spinning a few yarns in the Arnprior Mall.

"I had an old chum, a kind of a witty old lad, who was doctoring with a specialist," says Willard. "He got all togged up in his wedding and funeral suit one time to go to Ottawa. He was walking up the main street to the railway station, when he meets this lad who was always stickin' his nose into other people's business. When he saw him, my chum knew what was coming. The old lad would try to 'pick his business out of him'.

" 'Where are you goin' all togged up in your Sunday best?' asks the lad.

" 'I'm going to see my doctor,' my chum answered, figurin' 'I'll fix you, you empty-headed old busy body!'

" 'Doctor, eh? Doctor who? What would his name be?'

" 'Well now, his name happens to be Ray.'

" 'H-m-m-ph,' snorts the nosy lad, 'there's no Doctor Ray I know of in this town.'

" 'No, he's in Ottawa and a damn good man he is, too! They say,' says my chum, 'he's got turrible good eyes, so good he can see right through you.'

" 'He can, eh?' says the nosy lad. 'Now what would his full name be, then?'

" 'Well sir in the letter I got, it said, Please report to Doctor, X-Ray, Dept. C, 2nd Floor, Civic Hospital, Ottawa. So, I'm headin' out now to see Doctor X. Ray,' says my old chum as he walked away smilin'."

A HEAD OF STEAM

"Travellin's good for a lad, yuh know," says Willard. "Educative, if you know what I mean, and makes you feel kinda bigger inside."

"Food for your soul," commented his chum.

"Exactly! And yuh run across some comical things — like I was in Regina once, stayin' at the Plains Motel, corner of Albert and Victoria Streets. I met this doctor there from Portland, Oregon, and we took a wee tour 'round the Parliament Buildings. Then he says to me, 'Would you take a cool ale?'

"Says I, 'Well I'm not a drinkin' man but I suppose on a hot day I could handle one to offset the dehydration that could set in.'

"As we were goin' into the tavern, he gave me a kind of a nudge noddin' his head towards two ladies who had followed us in and sat down to the left and just behind us. They were good lookers and pretty fancy. There was an old lad sittin' next to them.

"Says this one lady to the lad, 'Would you like to go out?'

" 'Well,' says he, 'I don't think that would be too wise. You see I just came in.'

"Says she in a kind of sarcastic way, 'Aren't you a good sport, now!'

" 'Well,' says he, 'I have the radio, TV, and I read the sports page. Actually, I follow sports pretty closely.'

"I kept lookin' 'round at them," said Willard. "I suppose it was none of my business, but it was a kind of different situation than I'd see as a rule back home in Arnprior.

" 'Do you play?' she asked the lad.

" 'Well, just the radio,' says he.

" 'Dammit! Do you want to go out with me?'

" 'Oh, THAT!' says he. "I'm not a city lad and I guess I'm a wee bit slow at pickin' things up. But now that you put it that way . . . If you had come along last night — *maybe* — but you see, I enjoyed my nuptial obligations this morning already and at my age it'll take me boiler about three days to build up a head of steam to make the old locomotive whistle again!' "

TAKIN' 'ER TO THE LIMIT

I mind one time I met Willard on the main street. I hadn't seen him around for a while. "Gidday, Willard!" says I. "Where've you been?"

"Well sir now I just got back from a trip west. Drove my new half-ton out to give 'er a good run and try 'er out," he grinned.

"How far'd you go?"

"Well, I guess I went about as far as a fellah could go. I went clear out to the Pacific Ocean and kept goin' 'til the water got so deep I had to turn back."

"Well sir, Willard," I laughed, "nobody can say you didn't take 'er to the limit!"

HIGH ROAD TO WHITE LAKE

I was crossing through the bus station in Vancouver, one time, to catch a bus for the ferry to Victoria. Who do I see striding along, elbows swingin' and a brand new pair of braces over a chequered shirt, but Willard — as large as life!

"Gidday, Willard!" I yelled, from maybe 25 feet away.

He turned with a look of surprise. "Well I'll be goldanged! Isn't it turrah what you'll see when you haven't got a gun! It's Joe Mufferaw, himself!"

"Where the hell are you goin', Willard?" I asked.

"Well now to tell you the truth, it's time fer me oats and I was just goin' into this wee place to put on the nose bag. A lad gets hungry in the Western air. But, I'm flyin' out fer home tonight."

I was about late for my bus so I couldn't stay to chat. "Willard, when you get home would you phone my place and let them know I'll be leavin' Vancouver by bus tomorrow? I'll phone from Thunder Bay."

'I'll do that. You can depend your life on it. I'll tell them that you took the low road and I took the high road, so I got to White Lake before you!"

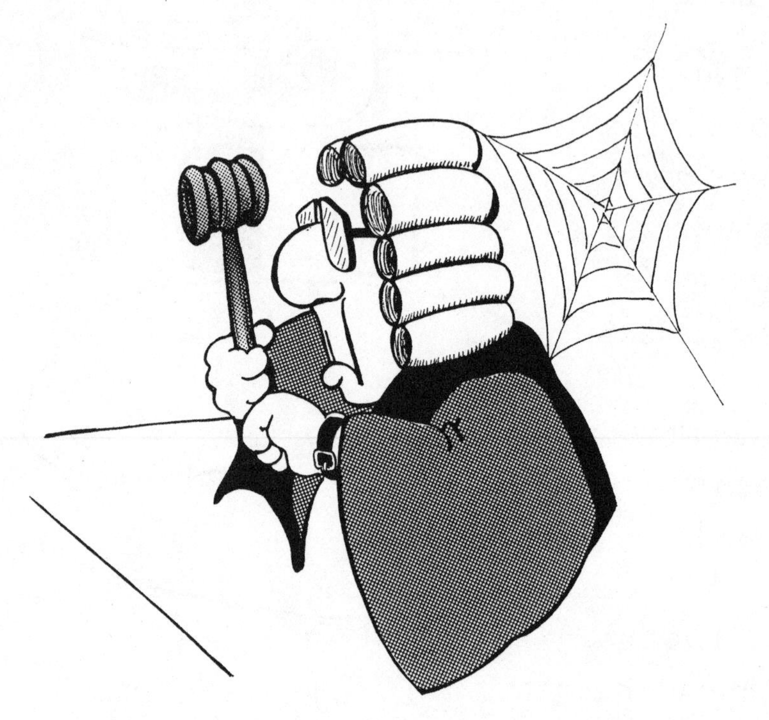

REGULAR ATTENDER AT COURT

Willard has one great obsession — attending courts in the area. He got started on this when a second cousin of his, a police sergeant, said, "Why don't you visit me in Carleton Place sometime and see what we do in court?"

"Ever since," says Willard, "I been a regular at court sessions. I'm always there before they commence and when they call criminal court, I get in quick to catch a seat.

"I'm in court so regular that one time I was late and at the recess the Judge says to me, 'I held court up as long as I could this morning, Willard, but finally had to start without you!'

"I had dinner with the Judge that day in the restaurant across the street and I apologized for being late, adding with a kind of a grin, 'I'm a busy man, you know, Judge. This retirement's a big job when you're not used to it!'

THE HOLDIN' CELL

"A police lad I know in Renfrew said to me one time, 'Willard, you see the culprits tried and sentenced in court all the time and kinda know how they feel. Would you like to see where we hold them while they think over their unlawful activities while they're waitin' on judgment to be passed on them?'

" 'Well, yes,' says I. 'I guess it would be good to see both sides of the question.'

"He took me to the holdin' cell, opened the door and when I leaned kind of over to look in, he gave me a shove, slammed the door, and blacked out the light. Scared the livin' daylights out of me, so he did.

"He soon turned the light back on and asked me, 'How'd you like that?'

" 'Well sir now there's a turrible shortage of daylight in there and furniture is pretty scarce but fortunately my holdin' time was short — and if you don't mind, I'll stick to givin' the Judge a hand and leave you to handle the pre-court appearance. One thing for sure, I'll be a better behaved citizen now I've experienced the grimmer side of your system

" 'I don't think I could make myself at home while I'd be waitin' in the holdin' cell. In fact, the most holdin' I'll be doin' from now on is holdin' me prayer book in church!'

"I was coddin' him a bit, yuh know, and didn't want him to know how close I'd come to messin' my drawers!"

SIXTY DAYS

"I mind everything I see," says Willard. "One time when I was travellin' west, I was in court in Moosejaw.

"This lad was up before the Judge and the Judge says, 'Why didn't you come in to court when you were supposed to?'

" 'Well,' says the lad, 'I was at a party the night before court day. I was kinda feelin' rough and tired that morning and my breath would have knocked a buzzard off a shit wagon, so I just decided not to come. I shouldn't o' stayed so long at the party.'

" 'Well sir now,' says the Judge, 'you'll be stayin' even longer at the party I'm going to send you to. I hope you enjoy it. How does sixty days in the County Jail sound to you?' he snapped and banged his gavel calling for the next case."

SMELLIN' LIKE ROSES

"Oh, I mind every little thing ever happened to me," Willard says, "and lots of things I mind are just as well not said.

"I've said more than my prayers and all of my sport hasn't been reported on the sports page. Mostly, people seem to like to chat with me and we have a few laughs. We always manage to add a wee bit of bullshit to a dry story to moisten it up and it comes up smellin' like a rose on a spring day!"

And I can't think of a better way to describe The Valley way of spinning yarns.

> 127

ENVOI: LAUGH AT YOURSELF

"If yuh can't laugh
at yourself,
then who can yuh laugh at?"
grins the back fence philosopher.

"Well, you, maybe,"
grunts his crabby neighbor.